I0711296
This Book Belongs To:

Copyright © 2021 by SEASONAL JOY PRESS

FIRST EDITION

CUPID
IS
Stupid

my cat
is
my
valentine

yer
still
single

Why fall in
LOVE
when you can fall
ASLEEP

TEAM
NO
Valentine

Coffee is my
Valentine

galentines
DAY SQUAD

I Love Me!

Single
AND
Loving it

happy
SINGLES
awareness
DAY!

february
14TH
JUST ANOTHER DAY!

At least my

dog loves me

in
LOVE
with
MYSELF

SALTY
but
SWEET

I HATE
YOU
THE LEAST

I believe
in love
at third
beer

Valentines day
SINGLE
and
fabulous

PIZZA IS MY
VALENTINE

YOU
are a good
reason to be
HAPPY

NO
CUPID
ZONE

WILL YOU BE MY
Valentine?
JUST KIDDING
I HATE
everyone

Be the
reason
someone
smiles
today

LOVE
with
all your
heart

BE
KIND

LOVE IS
in the air
try not to
BREATHE

HAPPY VALENTINES DAY
TO ME
I LOVE YOU

LOVE
BITES

SINGLE
and
FABULOUS

FIND
Something
you love
and do it
FOREVER

LOVE
DISAPPOINTING
PIZZA
IS ETERNAL